811
HAR

Harrison, David L.
(David Lee),
1937-

Bugs.

$16.95

30082000314429
10/28/2009

DATE			

bugs

bugs

poems about **creeping** things

David L. Harrison

DRAWINGS BY
Rob Shepperson

WORDSONG

HONESDALE, PENNSYLVANIA

To Jeff, Tim, Kris, Tyler, and Jon with love —D.L.H.

For Elizabeth —R.S.

Text copyright © 2007 by David L. Harrison
Illustrations copyright © 2007 by Rob Shepperson
All rights reserved
Printed in China
Designed by Helen Robinson
First edition
Second printing

Library of Congress Cataloging-in-Publication Data
Harrison, David L. (David Lee).
Bugs : poems about creeping things / David L. Harrison ;
drawings by Rob Shepperson. — 1st ed.
p. cm.
ISBN-13: 978-1-59078-451-8 (hardcover : alk. paper)
1. Insects—Juvenile poetry. 2. Children's poetry, American.
I. Shepperson, Rob, ill. II. Title.
PS3558.A6657B84 2007
811'.54—dc22
2006011586

WORDSONG
An Imprint of Boyds Mills Press, Inc.

815 Church Street
Honesdale, Pennsylvania 18431

Contents

bugs

Bugs moved under
my welcome mat.
If bugs can't read,
explain that.

I've always said
that bugs are pests,
but bugs who read
are welcome guests.

gn*at*

Once upon a
time
a gnat
donned a
sword and a
feathered hat.

"I'm tougher,"
he snarled,
"than any
rat!"

(which terrified
the neighbor's
cat).

But he went too
far,
this fearless
gnat:

He shook his
sword
at a passing
bat,

who opened
his mouth
and—
just like that—
swallowed him!

(all but the
sword
and the hat).

spiderwebs

Webs sparkle
on the lawn
like diamond
necklaces
at dawn.

Shiny droplets—
small oases—
beckon spiders
to their places.

Silently they
look and lurk.

Time now for
spider work.

a tick's friends

A tick has
no
friends.

Therefore,

my
story
ends.

millipede

Millipede
giggles
wherever
he goes.

Grass
tickles
all of those
toes.

w o r m

(FOR TWO VOICES)

(FIRST VOICE)	(SECOND VOICE: TRAFFIC)

Warn any
worm
you happen
to

HONK!

meet:
A worm should
never
cross
the

TOOT!

(FIRST VOICE)   (SECOND VOICE: TRAFFIC)

street.
When pavement's
hot
and cars
are
                              SCREECH!
fast,
a worm is
soon
a thing of
the
                              SQUISH!
past.

scorpion

Of all the things
I'd like to be,
a scorpion isn't
one of them.

But here's a tip
for you from me:
Be careful making
fun of them.

They have too many
scorpion tots,
every year a
ton of them.

You may like them
lots and lots,
but frankly I like
none of them.

fle*a*

A flea known as Ralph
swallowed a cow.
It's a mystery how.

And after the cow
he swallowed a horse
(a huge one, of course).

But with a giraffe
he ran out of luck.
Its legs got stuck.

It's impossible now
to understand Ralph
wif giraffe in hif mouf.

dragonfly

Dragonfly
and Snapdragon
planned to wed.

"No one thinks
our love affair
will last," they said.

"For a honeymoon,"
said Dragonfly,
"come fly with me.
I will show you
wondrous sights
beyond the sea."

"You're such a dear,"
his true love said.
"I can't, my sweet.
Alas, I have no wings
and only roots for feet."

"Don't cry," he said.
"I have a plan.
We leave at noon!"

And off they flew
for their honeymoon
in a red balloon.

grasshopper

Grasshopper:

downright
tacky—

chaws
weeds,

spits
tobacky.

grub

A grub
vacationing
at the ocean

slathers on
the suntan lotion.

Tender skin
can quickly
roast,

and sunburned grub
as charred
as toast

is not
a pleasant
notion.

b*ee*s

(FOR TWO VOICES)

(FIRST BEE)	(BEE CHORUS)
Bees	ZZZZZZZ
buzzing	ZZZZZZZ
	ZZZZZZZ
	ZZZZZZZ
in the	ZZZZZZZ
flowers,	ZZZZZZZ
	ZZZZZZZ
	ZZZZZZZ
sipping	ZZZZZZZ
nectar	ZZZZZZZ
	ZZZZZZZ
	ZZZZZZZ
by the	ZZZZZZZ
hours,	ZZZZZZZ
	ZZZZZZZ
	ZZZZZZZ
hurrying	ZZZZZZZ
while	ZZZZZZZ

(FIRST BEE)   (BEE CHORUS)

ZZZZZZZ

ZZZZZZZ

days are   ZZZZZZZ

sunny,   ZZZZZZZ

ZZZZZZZ

ZZZZZZZ

keeping ZZZZZZZ

bee-zy   ZZZZZZZ

ZZZZZZZ

ZZZZZZZ

making   ZZZZZZZ

honey!   honey!

praying mantis

Sits
mo-
tion-
less,
still,

like
   he's
      pray-
         ing,
            waits
               until

something
doesn't
see
him
there.

Lunch
at
once—

he's
said
his
prayer.

seventeen-year cicada

Cicada's grumpy,
red-eyed,
mean,
set his
alarm for
seventeen.

Noisy grubs
disturbed him
early.
Who can
blame him
for feeling
surly?

bookworm

Books
to us
are
food
for thought.

books
to him
are
thoughts
for food.

Bookworms
nibble
what
they
should not.

But though
we
think
the
bookworm's
rude,

plumpish bug

One day a bug
(a plumpish bug)
met a stick
(a walking stick)
who smilingly said,
"Let's have
some fun!"

The bug said,
"Thanks,
I've got to run!"

He met a lizard
(a long-tongued lizard)
who winkingly said,
"Come visit me!"

The bug decided
instead
to flee.

But then the bug
(that plumpish bug)
met a bug
as plump as he,
who gigglingly said,
"Let's play!"

That bug
(that fun and plumpish bug)
giggled back
and said,
"I think
I'll stay."

fly

(FOR TWO VOICES)

(FIRST VOICE)   (CHORUS)

That fly is dead!

                     You sure?

I smacked it with a
baseball bat!
After that
I jumped on it
from my bed.
It's dead!

                     You sure?

I pounded
on it
with a
book.
Go look.
I promise you,
that fly
is goo!

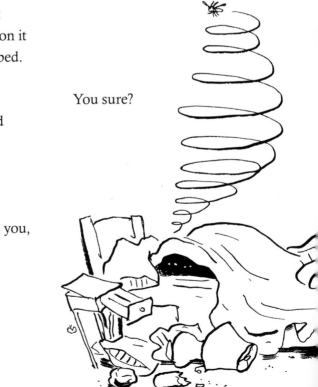

(FIRST VOICE) (CHORUS)

You sure?

I smashed it with a
rock.
Wham!
Bam!
That fly is history!
Gone!
Bye-bye!

You sure?

Why?

Because that fly
just
flew
away.

Have
a
nice
day.

cicada ghosts

Haunted skins
cling
emptily
to the rough bark
of the hackberry
tree,

and farther up
where I can't
see,
ghosts are
buzzing
eerily:
zz-zz-zz-zz
zeeeeee!

ants

I don't know
what they're looking for.

I don't know
what they'll find.

I do know
I feel nervous

with ants
on my behind.

caterpillar

A caterpillar
eats
until
it splits
its skin.

I tried that
once
at Thanksgiving—
but
never
again!

spider

In spider talk,
"I'm glad ta meeture!"

means

"I plans ta
catch and
eature
for a tasty
little treature!"

Don't go near
the nasty
creature!

du*m*b beetles

Two dumb beetles
set out to float
across the sea
in a tennis-shoe boat.

Sadly, the tennis shoe
sank before
the beetles had sailed
a foot from shore.

The beetles cried
with red faces,
"Duh, we shoulda
tied da laces."

lady*b*ug

Is it a
boy?

Is it a
girl?

To me
it looks
like
neither.

I wonder if
a ladybug

can
tell the
difference
either.

term*it*e

The termite
never eats
the way
he should.

It's not his fault.
His food
all tastes
like wood.

louse

The louse, I think,
should change its name
to something more sincere,

like Timothy
or Robin Lynn
or Pete or Guinevere

or Jeffrey Scott
or Jennifer
or Sandra Sue
or Klaus.

Who could ever
trust a bug
who calls *himself*
a louse?

centipede

Never kiss
a centipede
or pick him up
or hug him.

A centipede is
humorless;
all you'll do is
bug him.

In his youth,
the centipede
never learned
to play,

never learned to
hug or kiss.
Now he's
odd
that way.

So never kiss
a centipede,
I say
not once
but twice.

A centipede's
a waste of time.
He simply
isn't
nice.

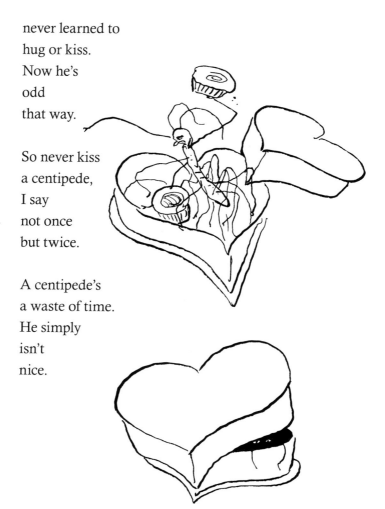

Spanish flea

(FOR TWO VOICES)

(DOG)   (FLEA)

He's a flea . . .

          a Spanish flea . . .

who's going to be
the death of me!

          Sí!

No one knows
how much I itch!

          I make the doggy
          scratch and twitch.

Sí!

He bites me here,

          I bite him there,
          I make him crazy

everywhere!

          Sí!

(DOG)   (FLEA)

I can't take it anymore!

                       Ah, that's very sad,
                       señor.

You're so awful!

                       I'm so bad.

Sí!   *Sí!*

chocolate-covered grasshopper

Me,
chew it?
Can't
do it!

m o t h

The moth is busy
all night long,
but does he make a peep?
No, he's too considerate
about our need for sleep.

So when we spy a drowsy moth
tucked in for the day,
shh, let's be
as thoughtful as he
and let him snore away.

apple worm

An apple a day
is a healthy way
to fight off germs ...

depending, of course,
on who is eating—
you or the worm.

*m*osquito

Have mercy!
I'm a poor mosquito!

Don't pull out
that can of DEET! Oh,

how I fear
your neighborhood!

I know you'd whack me
if you could!

Let's be friends!
Let's not fight!
All I ask is
one
small
bite.

bedb*u*g

(FOR TWO VOICES)

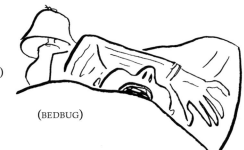

(VICTIM)   (BEDBUG)

Bad bug,

        bed bug,

sneaky little

        red bug,

rotten to the

        core bug,

scratch until we're

        sore bug,

claw until we're

        raw bug,

nip and chew and

        chaw bug,

bite us to the

        bone bug.

Leave our bed
alone, bug!

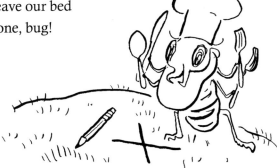

pi*ll* bug

Pill bug
on the floor
inside my door

can't decide,
now that he's in,
where to begin:

Doesn't like
the floor at all,
rolls in a ball,

catches a swift
broom ride
outside.

Adventure's over,
he's seen
the world:
It's flat.
It's wide.

no-see-um

No-see-um's
tiny bite

keeps you
scratching
half the night.

No-see-um's
no fun.

Next time you
don't see um,

run!

firefly

When your dimmer
grows
dimmer,
your glower
won't
glow,

your glimmer
won't
glim,
and your twinkler
is
slow,

dear little
firefly,
where
do you
go?

"Silly!
I go
to the
battery
sto'!"

bad beetles

Beetle hooligans
under rocks
wear smelly boots
and dirty socks.

They beat up bugs,
knock them flat,
cuss and yell,
things like that.

But toads take care
of bad beetles,
be they beegs
or be they leetles.

With one slurp
they gobble them …

"Urp!"

dung beetle

The
dung
beetle's
job
is
fine.

I'm
just
glad
it
isn't
mine.

roaches

(FOR TWO VOICES)

(FIRST ROACH)	(ROACH CHORUS)
We love your kitchen late at night.	
	We hate it when you flip the light.
We love to nibble this and that.	
	We hate it when you own a cat.

(FIRST ROACH)   (ROACH CHORUS)

We love it
when you
scream
and
yell.

We really hate
your
ROACH
MOTEL!

chigger

An elephant
would be
no match

for giant
chiggers
in a patch.

Since we have
to have the
chigger,

let's be grateful
he's not
bigger.

other bugs

I left out bugs
like thrips, earwig,
twig girdler, whirligig,
scurfy scale, and rabbit bot.

I thought them funny.

You might not.